Cowboys Vs. Chefs

Written by
W. G. White

Illustrated by
Xiana Teimoy

Chapter 1

"There's some garlic at the top of the hill, I promise!" said James as he climbed the steep hill. Behind him, his older brother Jeff huffed and puffed and grumbled. Jeff didn't want to climb the hill. Jeff wanted to buy regular garlic from the regular green grocers.

'Cowboys Vs. Chefs'
An original concept by W. G. White

Illustrated by Xiana Teimoy

Published by MAVERICK ARTS PUBLISHING LTD

Studio 11, City Business Centre, 6 Brighton Road,

Horsham, West Sussex, RH13 5BB

+44 (0)1403 256941

A CIP catalogue record for this book is available at the British Library.

ISBN 978-1-84886-865-6

Maverick publishing

www.maverickbooks.co.uk

Brown

This book is rated as: Brown Band (Guided Reading)

James was always dragging him off on foraging trips, looking for wild ingredients to go into food in their restaurant. But Jeff didn't think it was a good idea.

"No one forages for ingredients anymore, James," Jeff protested. "It's dangerous, dirty and much too sweaty." He wiped the sweat off his head and grumbled some more.

But James didn't care. He knew that all the real chefs went foraging. Fresh ingredients were vital to a good meal, and you couldn't get fresher than plucking it straight from the soil.

"You want to win the competition at the food festival tomorrow, right?" James asked, smiling as he reached the top of the hill.

"I'm really not bothered," replied Jeff.

"Well I do. And we're missing the black garlic: Head Chef's secret ingredient."

"Head Chef? Just call her Nana, you weirdo."

James grinned back at his sweaty, red-faced brother. From here, he could see the entirety of Rocky Road; his food-obsessed town. With more restaurants than homes and more chefs than *anything*, Rocky Road was every food-lover's dream.

Running through the middle of it all was the busy high street, with a clock tower at the end. All the best restaurants were found there. But tomorrow, that high street would host Rocky Road's Annual Food Festival.

A food festival with a competition. A competition with a prize. A prize of a five-course meal at the restaurant owned by Mr Scrummy, the mayor of Rocky Road. James could think of nothing better.

"There!" James exclaimed, pointing to a lonely, dead tree ahead of them. James rushed over and dropped to the ground beneath the tree, brushing some of the tall grass aside. Jeff wheezed along behind him.

"I told you I'd find some." James grinned proudly, then carefully scooped the soil up around the wild garlic. This was a special, black garlic that's usually made by cooking regular garlic over several weeks. It didn't grow naturally anywhere but here, in the sugar-sweetened hills of Rocky Road.

"Can we go now?" Jeff whined as James placed three whole garlic bulbs into his pocket. "We've still got to make the pasta, set up the stall, pre-dice the onions, and buy salt from Old Freda... I hate Old Freda."

"Yup, time to head back." James sniffed the garlic.

It was sweet and syrupy with hints of vinegar.

It was perfect.

Oh, they'd win tomorrow. James was certain.

Chapter 2

Next day, at the festival, there were stalls for every dish you could ever imagine. Perfect pizzas, colourful curries, beautiful burgers, saucy salads, luscious lasagnes, nourishing noodles, crispy chips, delicious desserts and many, many more.

James didn't know where to look. His eyes bulged and his mouth watered as he sniffed the tempting aromas. He dragged his feet as Jeff herded him through Rocky Road's busy high street towards their own stall.

“Would you hurry up!” Jeff grunted. “We’ve got loads to do!”

James wanted to stop and taste it all. He wanted a sip of Mrs Gravy’s beetroot and miso soup. A nibble of Chef Carotte’s flaky pesto tarts. A sniff of Mr Pain’s impressive ratatouille. It had perfect slices of plump tomato, aubergine, squash, and courgette.

There was some real competition here and James hadn’t even started cooking yet! There wasn’t any time to dawdle, he decided, as he rushed past Jeff.

“C’mon, Jeff! We’ve got a competition to win!”

They found their stall and were soon cooking up a storm. Jeff prepared vegetables as James got busy mixing the sauce and mashing the mushroom mince. They were cooking Head Chef Nana’s top-secret Bolognese.

As saucepans sizzled, frying pans hissed and chefs barked orders, a strange feeling settled over Rocky Road... as though a storm were coming. But not an *actual* storm. Worse than that.

"COWBOYS!" screeched Chef Dollop, as she pointed a bundle of floppy carrots down the high street. Sure enough, a gang of cowboys galloped towards them, lassos whirling above their heads and water pistols squirting at anyone in their way.

"Cowboys? In Rocky Road?" Jeff scoffed as he chopped a handful of fresh basil. "I don't believe it!"

As he spoke, a grubby cowboy with a tatty hat an[d] floppy moustache rode past, snatching the basil and stuffing it into a big sack.

"YEEE-HO-HO-HEEE,"

the cowboy hooted, turning his horse around and snatching the rest of Jeff and James's ingredients.

s shouted. “Give those back! We need ..’t cowboys say ‘yeehaw’?”

But the cowboy ignored James as he sped off, snatching ingredients from other stalls as he went, hollering incorrectly all the while. The same thing was happening all up and down the high street. Cowboys were snatching food left, right and centre. Before long, everything was gone and the cowboys vanished as quickly as they’d arrived, leaving the chefs of Rocky Road very confused indeed.

Chapter 3

"Now everybody be calm, please!" shouted Mr Scrummy. He stood as tall as he could, looking fancy with his official sash and chef's hat. Chefs and festival goers alike had gathered to complain; they wanted their food back and they wanted it now!

James and Jeff agreed. The cowboys had taken everything, even the black garlic. They'd cleared out every house, every shop, and every garden patch. There was nothing left at all!

The cowboys hadn't gone far, having made camp on the hill overlooking Rocky Road—the one with the dead tree. They'd started a fire and were dancing, eating and playing banjos with enthusiasm.

"How are we going to do the festival when the cowboys have all our dishes?" a man shouted from the crowd.

"My soufflé will be flat!" screamed another.

"I needed to glaze my parsnips!" The complaints kept coming.

"My cream will curdle!" And coming.

"Our potatoes needed seasoning!" And coming.

"Yes! Yes! I hear you!" Mr Scrummy struggled to make himself heard over the rabble. "I, too, was preparing to scramble my eggs. I understand your struggles, I do! Which is why Senior Chefs Ramsley

and Olivia and I are about to travel to the cowboys' camp and reclaim what is ours. It is our duty to face this fresh threat and remove it once and for all. Rocky Road's Annual Food Festival will continue as planned, I guarantee it!"

Once and for all? What did that mean? Had the cowboys been to Rocky Road before? James wasn't sure, but something about the cowboys had upset Mr Scrummy and the senior chefs.

James, Jeff and everyone in Rocky Road watched as Mr Scrummy, Chef Ramsley and Chef Olivia trekked through town and up the hill. The conversation between the chefs and the cowboys was short, and so far away it was impossible to hear, but James imagined it went something like this:

"Good gentle sirs," said Mr Scrummy, "you appear

to have acquired our food. Kindly return it and we can forget this ugliness entirely."

To which the cowboys most likely responded: "No."

James, Jeff and everyone in Rocky Road then watched as Mr Scrummy, Chef Ramsley and Chef Olivia were lassoed with a combination of rope and what must have been very strong spaghetti, tipped off their feet and rolled back down the hill.

"That went well," said Jeff. His tummy rumbled angrily.

Chapter 4

Mr Scrummy slunk shamefully back to town, and declared the situation hopeless. The cowboys were simply impossible to speak with. Too rough. Too tough. Too hungry. Instead, the mayor ordered the people of Rocky Road to search high and low for anything edible—anything at all—so that the competition could carry on.

James and Jeff searched as best as they could, but found nothing. No crumb, no sliver, no ounce of anything tasty, nutritious or appetising.

They shuffled back to the judges' table with heads hung and tummies rumbling.

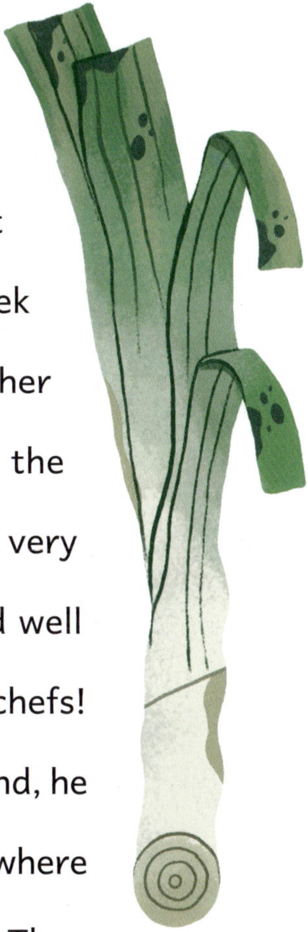

No one else had much luck either. In fact, the only thing tasty, nutritious, or even the least bit appetising was a single, skinny leek that Chef Olivia had been growing in her garden. As unimpressive as it was, the leek soon became the crown jewel in a very watery soup. A soup intended to feed well over a hundred hungry townsfolk and chefs!

As James queued with his bowl in hand, he stared up at the hill and the dead tree where the cowboys partied, danced and ate. They ate and ate and ate, stuffing their faces with the town's half-prepared meals and raw ingredients.

It was horrible to see. James couldn't stand it any longer. He dropped his bowl, grabbed Jeff by the arm, and yanked his startled brother in the direction of the hill.

"What are we doing?" Jeff asked, fear edging into his voice. "Where are we going, James? James, I want my leek soup. James, I'm hungry!"

"Me too, Jeff," growled James. "Hungry for justice."

Chapter 5

"I demand to speak with your leader!" James roared as he and Jeff arrived at the top of the hill. The cowboys' camp was a mess of apple cores, potato peels, pizza crusts and discarded spices. They'd eaten themselves to sleep, bellies full to bursting and mouths covered in sauce and grease. Yet, despite their gorging, the town's food was still stacked high, just waiting to be cooked.

"Demands, do ya?" hooted a cowboy wearing patchy overalls, a handlebar moustache hiding his upper lip.

"Hear that, boys and girls? Little thing be *demandin'!*"

Although they were asleep, the cowboys had enough energy to rock themselves awake with some mean-spirited laughter. And once they were awake, they started to eat *again*. Handfuls of dry pasta crunched between yellow, rotting teeth. Burgers were stripped of vegetables and devoured in a single bite. Rice was boiled until it was mushy and then seasoned with tomato ketchup.

"You're ruining it!" James cried. It was the most awful thing he'd ever seen. "You're eating all our food and you're doing it wrong!"

"I can't watch," squeaked Jeff, who covered his eyes and flinched at every *crunch*, *slurp* and *burp*.

"I demand to speak with your leader!" James repeated. And the cowboys continued eating. So

James kept demanding. And the cowboys kept eating. Until a grunt from a tent beneath the dead tree made the cowboys freeze.

"Now you've done it," said the overalls-wearing cowboy, whose name was Rodney. "Now you've really done it. You wanted to speak with the boss? Well here he is: Butch Badden."

The tent flaps peeled back and a hulking, grizzly man stepped out. He had more muscles than a gorilla, and almost as much hair. He wore a chequered poncho, a huge Stetson hat, and a pair of spurs on his boots shaped like pizza cutters.

"Speak," Butch growled, his eyes shaded by the brim of his Stetson.

Jeff, who was still covering his eyes, slipped behind James and quivered.

“I-I-I challenge you...” James began, feeling himself sweat and wondering if this was perhaps a bad idea. No. The town *needed* their food! “I challenge you to a duel, Butch Badden!”

The cowboys gasped, food frozen in their mouths. They looked between Butch and James, obvious fear and excitement buzzing around them.

“A cook-off at high noon,” James continued. “Under the clock tower. If I win, you and your gang return the food and you have to do the festival’s dishes every year. Forever.”

The cowboys gasped again, whipping their heads to face Butch for his reaction.

“I accept your duel, kid. But when I win,” Butch said, taking a heavy step forward, “you cook us a grand feast in our honour. Every year. Forever.”

Chapter 6

The high street was separated into two halves: chefs on one side, cowboys on the other and the clock tower between them. James and Jeff's workstation was on one side of the clock tower, Butch Badden's was on the other.

Chef Olivia, Chef Ramsley and two cowboys sat at the judging table in the middle. James noticed one of the cowboys was Rodney, the overalls-wearing one from the camp. They all wore blindfolds and had agreed to judge the competition on taste and taste alone.

"I'm still not sure about this," fretted Mr Scrummy. He hadn't been particularly happy when he'd heard of James's plan to save the town. In fact, he'd called it two noodles short of a stir fry—whatever that meant.

"We can beat him," James said as he and Jeff arranged their ingredients. The cowboys had agreed to return the Bolognese ingredients in the name of fairness. It was all there, even the precious black garlic. "After all, he's just a cowboy!"

Butch Badden arrived at his table, poncho whipping in the wind, revealing an array of professional chef's knives strapped to his belt. He grabbed a tomato from his basket, threw it into the air, and flourished a knife above his head. When the tomato landed on the table, it was in six perfect wedges.

James gulped. "Jeff, do something cool!"

Jeff—to his credit—tried. But it's hard to make peeling a carrot seem impressive.

The clock tower struck 12. High noon had arrived. The cook-off began.

Chapter 7

Flames burst into life as James added oil to his pan and sloshed it around. He threw in a handful of red onions and listened to them sizzling before sprinkling a pinch of salt and pepper over the pan.

Jeff hand-kneaded the pasta dough, before feeding it into a pasta machine and twisting the handle. Bundles of fresh spaghetti curled onto the table, all stringy and bouncy. They were added to a pan to be lightly boiled and Jeff returned to chopping vegetables.

On the other side of the street, Butch Badden was slicing vegetables with a finesse that James had never seen. He worked mushrooms into fine slices before pressing them into a neat shape.

Whatever he was making, it looked fantastic. How could a cowboy cook with such grace and style? James gritted his teeth and focused on his Bolognese. Head Chef Nana wouldn't be phased by a rival chef—James couldn't be either.

"I confuse you, don't I, kid?" Butch grunted. "Thought I'd be a pushover, right?"

"I'm cooking, thank you," replied James as he added chopped tomatoes and mushroom mince to his pan.

"I'm Rocky Road born and bred. Grew up with a whisk in one hand and a knife in the other. Used to be a chef here till they ran me out."

"You're lying..."

"Owned a nice little eatery; nothing special. Got me five stars too. Not that I did it for that. It were the smiles, kid. Did it for the smiles. Not everyone were smiling, mind you. Not the other chefs. Not the mayor." Butch sniffed and added a spinach sauce and an avocado to his mushrooms. "Said I were stealing customers. Makin' them look bad. Said I weren't welcome no more. I just wanted to make 'em smile, kid." Butch glared across at James and snarled, "Now? Now, I wanna make 'em cry."

With only seconds to spare, James and Jeff dished the spaghetti and Bolognese sauce onto a warm plate and carefully sliced the black garlic over the top. They finished it off with a couple leaves of basil and a side of home-baked garlic bread.

"Time's up!" declared Mr Scrummy as he rushed over to collect the dishes. "This better win," he snapped at James and Jeff before carrying the plate away.

Chapter 8

James felt like there was a lead ball in his stomach, and not just because he was nervous. If Butch's story was true, then Mr Scrummy and the senior chefs had run him out of town just for being a good chef. It wasn't fair. It wasn't right.

"First up," said Mr Scrummy as he presented Butch Badden's dish to the blindfolded judges, "is compressed wild mushrooms and avocado with spinach sauce." The judges were fed forkfuls of the dish by helpers.

"Eight out of ten," announced Chef Ramsley.

"Yeah, that's an eight," said the overalls-wearing cowboy as he smacked his lips and belched.

"Nine," said Chef Olivia.

"Nine," agreed the second cowboy with an added twitch of his head.

"Thirty-four points," announced Mr Scrummy, and the cowboys gave a silent celebration of pumped fists and excited hugging.

"Now, we have a black garlic Bolognese with homemade wheat pasta," said Mr Scrummy.

The judges tucked in again, and James's stomach twisted. Jeff hopped from toe to toe, his eyes clamped shut and fingers crossed. The entire town of Rocky Road held its breath as the scores were announced.

"Nine out of ten," declared Chef Ramsley.

"Nine," said Chef Olivia.

James glanced at the twitching cowboy judge and thought he spotted the man's eyes peeking out from below the blindfold. Could he see where the dishes had come from? "Six," spat the cowboy as he folded his arms. "The pasta's soggy. Where's the crunch?"

Again the cowboys celebrated silently whilst the townsfolk threw their hands up into the air in dismay. James's heart sank. There was no way to win now. They'd need a ten to tie with Butch, and Rodney was the only judge left.

He was, however, frozen with the fork lodged in his mouth. Unknown to anyone else, Rodney had been transported back to his distant homeland. In his mind's eye, he could see a boy sitting at his grandmother's table, legs swinging as he chomped happily on a bowl of Bolognese. Rodney then saw himself as a young man, bursting into the family's home and stealing the child's Bolognese. He'd escaped from three policemen and a mob of angry grandmothers to enjoy that Bolognese. It had been, and still was, his greatest crime.

"Ten!" Rodney tore off his blindfold and shovelled forkfuls of Bolognese into his mouth. "Ten!" He wept. "Ten!"

"Thirty-four," said Mr Scrummy. "It's a tie!"

"What the?! A tie? Y'all are being silly," shouted Butch, who marched over to the judge's table and shoved Rodney aside to get to the Bolognese. He lifted a forkful, sniffed it, squinted at it and then ate it. A moment later, his face lit up with a huge grin. "Well I'll be a salt shaker.

This is... this is **INCREDIBLE!"**

Butch laughed and rushed over to James and Jeff. "This is the best Bolognese I've ever tasted. Y'all gotta give me the recipe. Everyone has to try this! Everyone! Try the Bolognese, it's amazing!"

"But there's not enough to go around," said Jeff, and Butch stopped to look at the townsfolk and his small army of cowboys. Something shifted in his face, as though a weight were lifting from his shoulders.

He turned to his cowboys and said, "Bring these people their food. I've held onto my grudge for too long. I forgot what cooking's all about. It's about sharing. It's about the smiles."

Chapter 9

Rocky Road's Annual Food Festival was back on! But whilst the townsfolk danced, ate and cooked, James sat watching it all. Despite everything, he still felt bad. Everyone was having a great time, even the cowboys—even Jeff! But not James. No, James couldn't forget what Butch had said. And he couldn't let it lie either.

With his eyes set on Mr Scrummy, Chef Ramsley and Chef Olivia, James marched through the festival goers and said loud enough for everyone to hear,

"You need to apologise to Butch and give him his restaurant back."

The festivities died down as all eyes turned to James, the mayor and the senior chefs.

"Apologise for what, exactly?" asked Mr Scrummy, though the sweat on his brow showed he knew exactly what.

"For making him close his restaurant and bullying him out of town."

Mr Scrummy scoffed but Chef Ramsley and Chef Oliva looked away, ashamed.

Butch moved to stand behind James, his arms folded across his chest. "I wouldn't mind a sorry."

"You-you stole all our food!" Mr Scrummy seethed. "You're a thief!"

"He brought it back," said Jeff. "He fixed it. You didn't fix your mistake."

"I'm sorry, Butch," Chef Ramsley began. "I was jealous. It was wrong of me."

"I'm sorry too," said Chef Olivia. "I didn't even want to do it. It was David, really."

"My name's Mr Scrummy!" the mayor shouted. "Not David." He calmed himself and smoothed his sash. "But... very well. I see the error of my ways. Butch Badden, you have my apologies."

“And?” said James.

“And I love you?” Mr Scrummy shrugged and James rolled his eyes.

“No! Give him his restaurant back!”

“Oh!” he sighed. “Fine! Have it back. I don’t need it anyway.”

Butch smiled and squeezed James’s shoulder. “I’ll take the apology but y’all can keep the restaurant. I’m more a fan of the open road nowadays anyhow. But I wouldn’t say no to an annual festival booth... if y’all want me.”

“Of course we do,” said James.

“Alright! Now, let’s eat!”

And they did. Chefs and cowboys mingled, ate, played festival games and ate some more. And it was absolutely, ridiculously delicious.

Discussion Points

1. What is James foraging for in the beginning?

2. Who is the mayor of Rocky Road?

a) Mr Scrummy

b) Chef Olivia

c) Butch Badden

3. What was your favourite part of the story?

4. Where does James find the cowboy leader?

5. Why do you think Rodney gave James and Jeff's Bolognese a ten?

6. Who was your favourite character and why?

7. There were moments in the story when James had to be **brave**. Where do you think the story shows this most?

8. What do you think happens after the end of the story?

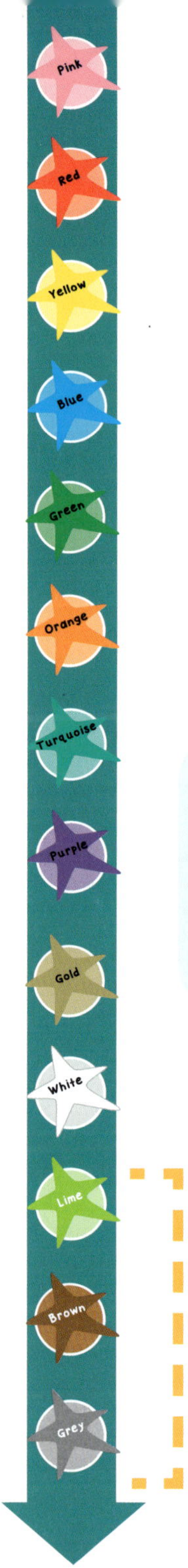

Book Bands for Guided Reading

The Institute of Education book banding system is a scale of colours that reflects the various levels of reading difficulty. The bands are assigned by taking into account the content, the language style, the layout and phonics. Word, phrase and sentence level work is also taken into consideration.

The Maverick Readers Scheme is a bright, attractive range of books covering the pink to grey bands. All of these books have been book banded for guided reading to the industry standard and edited by a leading educational consultant.

To view the whole Maverick Readers scheme, visit our website at

www.maverickearlyreaders.com

Or scan the QR code to view our scheme instantly!

Maverick Chapter Readers

(From Lime to Grey Band)

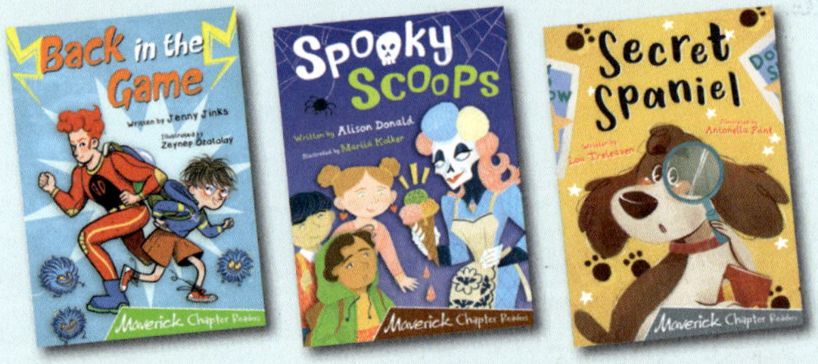